Find "new ways to see," just like Wink.

Kevin Lakes

Wink

by
Kevin Lakes

Illustrated by Marilyn Curry

Tell them, dear, that if eyes were made for seeing,
then beauty is its own excuse for being.

- Ralph Waldo Emerson, "The Rhodora"

In the Country of the Blind, the one-eyed man is king.

- H. G. Wells, "The Country of the Blind"

Dedication

To all horses. In many respects,
the foundation of the civilization
in which we live was built on their backs.
May we learn to appreciate their generosity to humankind,
and properly care for their descendants.

I was born in a field not far from the sea.

Salt air filled my nose and made me feel free.

A nuzzle from my mother,

a nudge from a man,

Some wobbles and stumbles,

in a few days, I ran.

From a family of winners, not a care in sight.
A racehorse I'd be, under bright lights.

Hope in the air, I was named Ride the Magic.
But a twist and a turn, and the moment turned tragic.

A spin, a sprint, and a slip in the rain.
A ping! A pop! and a piercing pain!

My world took a turn, dimming light from the sun.
Daybreak with two eyes, but now, only one.

So young and so injured, what would be my fate?
My potential was pierced when I slipped near the gate.

My eye was gone. What would happen to me?
From this point on, I'd learn new ways to see.

As dark as molasses in crescent moonlight
My coat was brilliant; what a beautiful sight!
I was still handsome (we all have some scars).
A beautiful head with a shiny white star.

Off to the racetrack! I was born to run.

Sandra, my trainer, made it all fun.

A man shaped my feet, he was called Billy.
Always trying to win, though at times it seemed silly.

Loving the races, with something to prove,
The crowds were all cheering. I made my feet move!

Four legs, two lungs, one eye—just think!
I fluttered my eyebrow and became known as Wink.

Riding the magic from course to course
All over the land, no finer horse.

I wasn't the fastest, far from the best,
But I never compared myself to the rest.

My racing days ended; the wins did not last.
What's a racehorse to do when his legs won't go fast?

Big questions, no answers. Then out of the blue
A family came along who knew just what to do.

Their idea made them smile, as I could see.
It was good for them. Was it also good for me?

We flew down the road, cutting air like a knife.
Where the moving stable stopped would determine my life.

I stepped out in the country, surrounded by trees.
A new friend named Odin and people to please.

Along came sweet Lola with friendship and cheer,
A wee little dog, whose ears could not hear.

Horses and dogs: best friends night and day,
We stick together with little to say.

At night, owls hoot and the seaside glistens.
Odin watches for me, and for Lola, we listen.

I have a new life trotting the roads.
Green grass every day and hauling small loads.
A family to live with, here is the key:
It's not how you look, it's what you choose to see.

About **Wink**

Wink is the nickname of Ride the Magic, a standardbred harness racehorse born in 2010 near Baddeck, Nova Scotia. Wink injured his eye as a foal and was later treated by veterinarians at the University of Prince Edward Island. Wink was raised to a yearling by a kind gentle man named Stewart MacRae. He was then acquired by Sandra Foley who trained him to race despite his missing eye. **Wink** recorded his best winning time at Bangor Raceway, pacing a winning mile in the time of (2:00.4) on the half-mile track.

Wink currently lives in a barn, runs in a field, and trots under harness on a road in the Annapolis Valley meters from the Lakes family home at Birch Hill. Wink is often visited by students from local schools who read his story and enjoy his personality. He never fails to engender respect, admiration, and empathy when he greets them with his innate confidence and playful nature.

About **Standardbreds**

Wink is a registered standardbred. This original breed was developed in the United States and Canada in the 19th century. The foundational sire was an English thoroughbred named Messenger. His progeny were bred with other breeds and types to produce speedy trotters and pacers for the roads and tracks of developing colonies.

Possessing a smooth gait, stamina, and exceptional toughness, they began as the common person's transportation option, also serving as companions and racehorses. With the invention of the motor vehicle, standardbreds transitioned to athletes of even greater speed, smoothness of gait, and beauty. They were admired and wagered upon at country fairs and large metropolitan tracks alike.

As the breed became faster, the world urbanized, and a horse under harness became a novelty. Large crowds diminished as the breed improved with many fans literally turning their backs from the horses as gambling options multiplied at so called "racinos," or casinos at the racetracks. The races continued at fewer and more competitive tracks.

Presently, the most vibrant racing and training regions are in Ontario, Prince Edward Island, Ohio, Pennsylvania, Indiana, Maine, New York, New Jersey, Florida, Scandinavia, Australia, France, and New Zealand. A North American original with attributes that are far from standard, the standardbred continues to bring enjoyment and inspiration to those that care for them and watch them compete.

About **Sandra**

Sandra Foley is a native of St. John's, Newfoundland. She developed a passion for harness racing after graduating from Dalhousie University, where she played Varsity Volleyball. For the last thirty-seven years, Sandra has not missed a single day at the barn caring for her horses. With 184 wins to her credit, Sandra is well known in New Brunswick racing for her competitive horses and caring nature. Her most prestigious win came when her hometown horse Big Bucks Bomber won the Walter Dale Memorial in 1990, breaking the "Curse of Walter Dale" as the first locally owned horse to win the event in its thirty-five-year history.

About **Billy**

Billy Watts is a well-known trainer and driver in Fredericton, New Brunswick. From a family of horsemen, with roots in Prince Edward Island, he continues to work with horses daily as a trainer and farrier. Billy's sense of humour, easy laugh, and memories of races gone by are typical of the best personalities the racing world makes possible.

About **Odin**

Odin is a member of the Lakes family and lives with **Wink** at Birch Hill. He is a brown-eyed mixed breed dog who keeps a close eye on the comings and goings. Although they are aware of their bias, the family often refers to Odin as the best dog ever.

About **Lola**

Lola is a French Bulldog that lives close to **Wink** and visits him whenever she can. Lola was born deaf, and she enjoys seeing and sniffing Wink's stable at Birch Hill.

About the **Author**

Growing up, **Kevin Lakes** spent his summer days and evenings on the backstretch of Fredericton Raceway, a few blocks from his home. With his father Eric, Kevin raced horses during a vibrant 1980s era of racing at the historic oval, training 132 winners. He has lived in Wolfville, Nova Scotia since 1994 while teaching at King's-Edgehill School. Along with his wife Penny and their sons, they have provided a home for a retired standardbred since 2003.

About the **Illustrator**

Marilyn Curry grew up near Newmarket, Ontario. She has lived her adult life in Boston and Nova Scotia, where she and her husband, Rev. David Curry raised their three children. She recently retired after 15 years as the Librarian at King's-Edgehill School in Windsor, Nova Scotia. A self-taught artist, she now has more time to pursue her passion for animals, gardening, family, and drawing. She visits Wink on a regular basis at his forever home, as she is always looking for new ways to see.

 FriesenPress

One Printers Way
Altona, MB R0G 0B0
Canada

www.friesenpress.com

Edited by Susie DeCoste

Photograph courtesy of Zach Lakes Productions

ISBN
978-1-03-915523-7 (Hardcover)
978-1-03-915522-0 (Paperback)
978-1-03-915524-4 (eBook)

1. JUVENILE NONFICTION, ANIMALS, HORSES

Distributed to the trade by The Ingram Book Company